THE SHADOW OF THE OBJECT